Tom Paulin was born in Leeds in 1949 and grew up in Belfast. He was educated at the universities of Hull and Oxford, and is Professor of Poetry at the University of Nottingham.

# WALKING A LINE

## Tom Paulin

*faber and faber*
LONDON · BOSTON

First published in 1994
by Faber and Faber Limited
3 Queen Square, London, WC1N 3AU

Photoset in Sabon by Wilmaset Ltd, Birkenhead, Wirral
Printed in England by Clays Ltd, St Ives plc

© Tom Paulin, 1994

Tom Paulin is hereby identified as author of this work in accordance with
Section 77 of the Copyright, Designs and Patents Act 1988

A CIP record for this book is available from the British Library

ISBN 0-571-17081-1

2 4 6 8 10 9 7 5 3

For Giti, again

# Acknowledgements

Some of these poems have appeared in: *Casablanca, Grand Street, Guardian, Honest Ulsterman, Independent on Sunday, London Review of Books, Observer, Poetry Review, Sunday Times, Times Literary Supplement.* 'A Belfast *Bildungsroman*' was originally published in the programme for the first production, by the Field Day Theatre Company, of Stewart Parker's *Pentecost.* 'Portnoo Pier' was originally published in the programme for the first production, by the Abbey Theatre, of Brian Friel's *Wonderful Tennessee.* I am grateful to Michael Hofmann and James Lasdun for asking me to contribute to *After Ovid: New Metamorphoses.*

# Contents

Steering north-eastward from the Crozetts, we fell in with vast meadows of brit, the minute, yellow substance, upon which the Right Whale largely feeds. For leagues and leagues it undulated round us, so that we seemed to be sailing through boundless fields of ripe and golden wheat.

On the second day, numbers of Right Whales were seen, who, secure from the attack of a Sperm Whaler like the Pequod, with open jaws sluggishly swam through the brit, which, adhering to the fringing fibres of that wondrous Venetian blind in their mouths, was in that manner separated from the water that escaped at the lip.

As morning mowers, who side by side slowly and seethingly advance their scythes through the long wet grass of marshy meads; even so these monsters swam, making a strange, grassy, cutting sound; and leaving behind them endless swaths of blue upon the yellow sea.

HERMAN MELVILLE, *Moby Dick*

## Klee/Clover

Nightwatch after nightwatch
Paul Klee endured
'horribly boring guard duty'
at the gasoline cellar
and every morning
outside the Zeppelin hangar
there was drill then a speech
tacked with junk formulas
he varnished wings
and stencilled numbers
next to gothic insignia
a private first-class
with a lippy dislike
of their royal majesties
and *Flying School 5 (Bavaria)*

he wrote home to Lily
*it's nice this spring weather*
*and now we've laid out a garden*
*between the second and third runways*
*the airfield's becoming*
*more and more beautiful*

each time a plane crashed
– and that happened quite often
he cut squares of canvas
from the wings and fuselage
he never said why
but every smashed biplane
looked daft or ridiculous
halfjoky and untrue
– maybe the pilots annoyed him?
those unlovely aristos
who never knew they were flying
primed blank canvases
into his beautiful airfield

# History of the Tin Tent

During the first push on the Somme
a temporary captain
in the Royal Engineers
– Peter Nissen a Canadian
designed an experimental
steel tent
that could be erected
from stacked materials
by an NCO and eight men
in 110 minutes

so the Nissen hut is the descendant
and enriched relation
of the Elephant and other
similar steel structures
that were adopted then adapted
for trench warfare

sheets of corrugated iron
beaverjoints purlins joists
wire nails and matchboard lining
were packed into kits
so complete societies
could be knocked and bent
into sudden being
by a squad of soldiers with a truck

a few tools
and a pair of ladders

barracks hospital
mess hall and hangar
— chapel shooting-range petrol dump *&c*
they were all bowed into shape
from rippling thundery
hundredweight acres
of sheet metal
Europe became a desert
so these tents could happen
though they now seem banal
like the word *forever*

all over England
on farmland and airfields
these halfsubmerged sheds
have a throwaway permanence
a never newpainted
sense of duration
that exists anywhere
and belongs nowhere
— ribbed basic
set fast in pocked concrete
they're almost like texts
no one wants to read
— texts prefabs caves
a whole aesthetic in reverse

# Linda Nicklin

Even as we sat together
in the very first class
I knew she came from a place
— meaning a warp of culture
some ideal actual space
I'd never actually been near
at least not on this side
of the Irish Sea

and so without desire
with a frugal disinterest
I began to draw a picture
— touching and naïf
of a market town in Lincolnshire
that she didn't want to leave
the draper's shop
where she bought those skirts
that geranium frock
the jackets like school blazers
— two pubs a chapel
a skewed spire
and some brick houses
in each interior
the alum verities of dissent
— starchcoloured wallpaper
a view of Mablethorpe
maybe the Authorized Version

– it was dull
it was a bore
no crack
no folklore
and all the while the enormous
flat wheatfields went on
and on . . . I imagined more
and then I didn't
for at 18 you don't want
that awful middle-England stasis
– the Saxon handpainted names
on each glazed shopfront
the hardware the bakery
those unbearable empty
shimmering crazed landscapes
where every road says simply
*there's no escape*
*stay decent stay here*
– but she'd caught a bus fifty miles
into the next county
and now I'm unpicking a guilt
about working her name
into a thin realist
irrecoverable timespot
a sort of lifesculpture
– with her definite chin
her short dark hair
that almost parched skin
she could have been
a kind of weekly cousin

whose name rang true
like the milled rim on a coin
as it hit-hits the counter

# The New Year

Because it's next door
to Blenheim Palace
– that hollow stagey
sandstone hatbox
this screened mansion
ought to be called Malplaquet
and the next one down
Ramillies
– a doucer name than either
but so what?
I don't care
about the War of the Spanish Succession
these estates
or their loyalty to the crown
and the latest drugrelated
offence by a member
of the Marlborough family
leaves me cold
– but as I walk with friends
past enfiladed trees
here in the tame Cotswolds
it's not the office plot we're seeding
that makes me anxious
– not the way the pheasants cronk
in this chill demesne
its tiny Tibetan deer its folly
the fake Roman bridge

– it's not these I think
that worry me
but my own language
my one language
where each word
strains to utter itself
like a mallety wooden turd
– and just as these trees
are only half a wood
so every sentence
builds itself
on a kind of clearance
builds itself on risk
and an ignorance
of what's been hacked down
or packed up
– I'll go back home after a while
like a malefactor
a lost soul who's stared
into a false battlefield
or that tight terrible hollow
in Gibbon's prose style

# Matins

A tinniness in that bell
– I was ten when I heard it first
its sad but urgent tang
binging across two dead –
you could hardly call them fields
and there it goes again
off-key but beating out
its meek unsettled belief
on a shore of this small republic
not a *cloche fêlée* for sure
just Anglican Irish and poor

maybe I'll cross those acres
– deadness and brambles just
between our house and the church?
go into that half-strange porch
its odour of damp and limewash
strawbottomed chairs and slack
well loose little case of hymnals
it must be a tribal thing
this wanting to go back there
(d'you want to kneel in prayer?)
this wishing the words were firm
with a bit of a kick and a skip
why couldn't they stay the same
and sing *bing-ding bing-ding*?

# The Lonely Tower

'WANTED — *coastal farm, site, derelict house, period house, stable yard, outhouse, lodge, martello. Must be on sea. Immediate cash settlement. Box Z0490.*'

Either incognito and desperate
or more likely a small developer
dreaming the obvious
they've neither the form nor the substance
only the theme
but what a theme it is
— John Melly's breezeblock bothie
in the dunes above Dooey Strand
a windy look-out post
from the Emergency
the Lone Man's House
at Ballyeriston
(baled hay in every room
blank uncurtained windows
dust sealight bullocks blurping in the fields
doggy bones on the kitchen floor)
that coastguard station
— roofless since the state's founding
set on the hillside
above Portnoo Post Office
an entire deserted village even
where the road gives up its potholed ghost
in a wilderness of scree and ironstone

– from the dead martello
down to the shed on the cement pier
most any building
in this squally clachan
could quicken into newness
– you can write them out in a verse
or jump in a lorry
rammed with cement and timber
then *bash bash bash* till the day
when you paint *Wavecrest* on the gatepost

# Painting the Carport

It was a stretched bungalow
not the kind of building you'd assent to
– at least not easily –
for what existed in the picture window
was somehow buoyant and untrue
– the rotary clothesline flymowed lawn
sky its usual icy blue
a hedge of instant fillingstation conifers
satellite dish and silky mastiff
chained to a bunker

this was the dogsleep I was coming out of
my petty *crise* my *quarantaine*
everything to do with being stuck
in the same job in the same place
but here I'd woken in another fiction
where the man who owns this unreal view
– let's call him Jacklin –
will take my arm and talk
about the doubleglazing he's installed
but he binds on and on he bores me solid
so I watch the conifer quicks and listen
for the *chuck chuck chuck* of an ambush somewhere

*C'mon* he says *you've been this way before*
*it's your own private space this*
*Calvin's English republic*
I turn and ask him *Jacklin*
*where is it that we're heading now?*
*Dunno* he says *but Tom I tell you this*
*at the end of the day*
*dot dot dot has got to happen*

# Middle Age

Maybe the true taste of it
is knowing the limits of your own fraudulence
– that'll do for a precept
you can either frame the thing
or spray it on the wall
of that sunny little turdshrine
called *My Personal Wisdom*

but what's waiting out there
is some stretched invisible cordon
– it's like I found this credit card
and perfected a signature
I don't think it's mine though
and neither do you

# The Firhouse

There's nothing else handy
only this bit of blottingpaper
I'm trying to make notes on
with a gummy fountain pen that either dries or blurs
as if it knows this poem (if it *is* a poem)
will never quite get written
but right now I have to put down something
about this curious house off a main road
maybe a mile or so from a dormitory village near Gotham
(bit sinister that name but it's better than Bunny)
the house is set next a clump of fir trees on a small hill
and looks out over a wide flat valley
where nothing much ever happened

it has coppercoloured rooftiles
that seem like they're made of baked felt
the walls are cream snowcem
and the roof's pitched just a shade too steep
though you could say the angle of it
echoes the shape the fir trees make
– diagrammatic like the TV aerial
clamped tight to the sentrybox chimney
a roofslope cut into by the Velux window
that makes another angle when it's opened

whoever built this liked squares and triangles too much
and they were obsessed by fussy additions –
the outbuildings are a mess permanently unfinished
like furry shoeboxes stuck together
the rosebushes are packed tight the way they are in a nursery
the garden's jammed with overgrown Christmas trees
and webby fernspray cypresses
a sign at the far end says CONIFERS ➤

isn't there something strained something perky but daft
about this bit of rural real estate this homey place of business
like a pocket telephone exchange out on its own
but warmed and protected by the fir trees?
there's a dormobile parked to one side
and hosepipe trailing across the lawn like a cable
planes land in the airport down in the valley
cropsprayers floom over huge fields of yellow rape
there's a big bendy river
and on summer days all the colours come out loud and clear
like a Festival of Britain painting
I've been sitting here for the last half-hour
in my muddy VW
watching the house from the lane
– it has a sign by the gate saying *Keeper's Cottage*
and now I feel like a man obsessed with the woman who lives
    there
a man who should be at work and either feels guilty
or looks suspicious or is somehow out of place

there she is at the kitchen window washing dishes
while I'm inventing an excuse to call

*— D'you sell conifers?* I ask when she opens the door
she's fortyish with pale skin and sisalish hair
wears a grey mohair jumper eyes blue
a speck of yellow sleepyolk in the left one
*— Conifers!* she laughs *oh we used to —*
*I keep telling my husband to take that silly sign down*
*— He's given up on the trees?*
*— We stopped them last winter there just wasn't a market*
*— I'm sorry to bother you now*
she forces a smile and shuts the door


walking back to the car it's like I'm on the edge of a secret
something to do with a closed door and the word *they*
a sort of riddle
who was it said *take it from me son*
*they never invite you in?*
but why should you want in? why should there be
some little *puja* room you have to come inside of?
only there's times you notice some slight subtle difference
in the emotional weather
a cut-off point or an absence
because really you're a stranger and who wants a stranger
in their own house?
from now on in
I'll be writing in a vacuum about a vacuum
*— there's no such thing as society*
*only men and women living together*
*on the great open site of human freedom*
so in the east midlands of England
you'll find the first and last frontier
and then face the question — could anyone write it?

# L

Tongue *lingua*
it enters small apertures
that are hairy wet waxy
or taste of old hapennies
the kind you sucked as a kid
or laid out on a railtrack
so the train to Helen's Bay
could punch them into sharp haloes

often it relishes
the faint kidney flavour
of some defunct sandstone *pissoir*
behind overgrown bushes

in undercover skirmishes
it acts as love's secret agent
a diligent sapper that digs
into ears and emery armpits
or slides between fingers and toes

it penetrates the bum on state occasions
and searches the *mons pubis*
for a fleshy button
a tiny wee *cep*

*plink plonk* it endures the juice of scallions
and longs to slither
into a left nostril

like a heifer drawn to the rocks
it loves to lick salt
and dwell on the sea's minerals

with a fur of tannin on it like a mole
and hiding a soft saggy underbelly
this tongue thing's a supple instrument
kinda decent and hardworking
and often more welcome than the penis
– too many poems speak for that member
maybe it's time I unbuttoned my tongue?

# Almost There

If you'd written it out a couple more times
or even hit it a kick
you'd have cracked the thing
– as it is
there's a kind of glitch
in what you're saying

that tar and felt shack on the headland
is windy with our belonging
but the speechjolt
its wet spark
is travelling still
travelling through darkness and moisture

# Unnatural Object

*(for David Hammond)*

In the clearly clearly light
I'm happening to stare up
at the slopes of Croagh Patrick
– maybe something's changed
since I was a kid
and walked the shores of Clew Bay?
or is it simply a trick
of the running light?
because what I see far above me
right at the very top
is a tiny white bungalow
on a magnificent site
– I know this must sound
just a mite unhinged
for it can't be a bungalow
can't be a holiday home
it's a quite other building
now I remember you saying
that meets all the barefoot
bleeding pilgrims instead
– a snowcem and breezeblock basilica
with microphone loudspeaker
and a purply perspex blister
like the rear turret
on a Lancaster bomber

*– o little hollow*
*little kitschy box*
*who plonked your concrete*
*among the rocks*
*on Patrick's mountain?*
*or have you sneaked*
*out of a novel by Paul Gallico?*

# Macaulay Jail

I am writing from Wireless Colony
about prisons and prisoners
jails have been overcrowded for long
and as well as convicts are undertrials
– alleged anti-socials many student
awaiting court verdict
and languishing in cells
– why not government grant amnesty these people
and release them on Christmas Eve
or New Year Day
so they can breathe fresh air again
so they can maybe start new life?
I say retreat from reality will not help
in keeping at bay from shadow of poverty
I am never hopeless in saying this

## ਕਸ਼ ਨਹੀਂ

*Cush*
with an aspirate *n* at the end
so *cushnəi*
which might be a silk cushion
meaning *nothing*
or as you would take
zero nil nought
nix nowt fuck all
even love duck or no score
wrap them in the lightest scarf you can find
then chuck the bundle away

this could be scanning a recipe
for a pretend morsel
on a wide green leaf
a way of waiting
almost with prayer and fasting
for the main course

or it could be a pouffe from Turkestan
a word out of Sanskrit
that means *something-not*
it's love in an arranged marriage
or love in a love marriage
a song in Hindi that asks
why did you leave me with my desire?

I want to take this sound with me into Zion
or I want to put Zion into nothing
– like lances or prayer flags
the long sticks of sugar cane
hide all that's uncrushable
– uncrushable and not knowable
– not the sticky brown jaggery sweet *ghurr*
but the unsticky unbrown etc

it's like that story where Saladin
gets the better of Richard Lionheart
or like the difference
between a scarf and a heavy sword
or between
– air and morality
   art and the law
   deepblue and the devil
so many fatuous binaries
and all
to too much purpose

I lift its letters
out of a closed lidless box
a floppy bin
– why so floppy *bin*?
for aren't I a brisk confident kind of male person?
– not falorie
   not falorie
   no never
I can flex my muscles and fix things

so I open this soft bin
and take out
ਕ and ਮ
it's like a selfassembly kit
this alphabet
that asks you to hang its letters out
from the line above
as though each one was a decoration
clicked to a wire

I may be less than expert
in the sign system they call Gurmukhi
but this is my big chance
to observe a state of total ignorance
– all that I'll never never know
and the little I will

in this upholstered void
there's a feathery ottoman
a goose
that's plump neckless
and pretend tame
– I sit on it and fail
either to know or to think

Lord why did you plant me in dreamtime
and then let me melt?
why did you say
this is a pierless bridge you're travelling
that ends in space ocean air
it's that little matchstick trestle

in *On Through the Silent Lands*
— the rawpaint plain
river
and haunted pilgrim

he's slinking down from the mountain
an old man in a dark suit
that's as shiny as an elbow patch
— he clutches a bowler hat
as though he's a tired member
of some ruined L.O.L.
a brother who's walked away from the Field
so many long miles
he holds his bowler sadly
as you might a book or a satchel
maybe his sword lies broken
in some birdless corrie
or behind a betting-shop
on the Ormeau Road?
let's call him Dick
Mr Richard Crossan
an outofwork actor
or a bankrupt pigfarmer
walking down towards the bridge

not the dream of becoming
nor the dream of belonging
but the dream of Being

*cushnəi* may be dovesong
a *roucoulement*
brimming in the poplars
these gizzly light-torn poplars
round a walled farm
that has a tubewell
two water buffalo
and a pile of green fodder
in the courtyard

I lie on a string bed and listen
to the nothing that is not there
and the nothing that is
– water and light
  leafsong
  three lizards clamped to the wall
  a *ghazal* on the radio

and if you believe
just saying this
must be easy written
well it isn't
for I've been walking across a kind of desert
forty-three years four months
and eleven days
looking for the seed
of this tiny world
a world that doesn't add up

I found it last Sunday
(5/7/92)
the date's exact
because like Bishop Ussher
I want to frank
the day of creation
and post it to its posterity
– try to do that though and it shows
you can't be the full shilling
either that or the entire shimmering universe
is just another Anglo-Irish folly
but if you don't believe it's nothing
then you're well on the road
to dates and definitions
to a spot in time
where some scabby crusader
takes his sword to a silk scarf
– you hear him cry out
*it's not true*
*that I'll never never know*
*what I never never knew*

# Wisdom's Dark Grove

*Svakde   amrit vela*
it's dayclean – the dawnlight –
and they're crossing a field
behind the walled farmhouse at Lakpur
three women in saris
one's holding a toilet roll in her left hand

they'll squat in a grove of sugar cane
their dark latrine
then walk back joking – *leh!* –
like nuns who've been released
from the flesh's burdens

# Kevin O'Higgins and the Justice Squad

It has joined the nations of the earth
but the old people in this baby state
they whisper *are we fit to govern?*
*lookit those swaddlers in their twenties*
*they've taken us over*

such a struggle to get born – blood in buckets
*bang! whang!* the gun and the scaffold
and then to be abandoned like this!
left like Oedipus in a handbag
with no one to find us or call us worthy

so new state new uniforms a same old street
paved with bricks its rooftops watched
icecream parlour a classical doorway
and – for this is the second big
state funeral – the male mourners in uniform

tomorrow those four will agree
to shoot four other youths each dawn
volley after volley in the jail they own
*personal spite! vindictiveness! great heavens!*
*one of those men was a friend of mine!*

## 51 Sans Souci Park

I wake early in their new flat
– my parents' flat off the Malone Road
wake to an unremitting a constant sound
six inches above the roof
– a batty churgle
a frantic mishmash
that's the entirely usual noise
of an army helicopter
– usual but this time worse
than ho-ho normal
because a gong is sounding
inside my head already
*you sinned with drink dong!*
*you sinned with drink bong!*
so an armed flying machine
is way inside my head
inside a strange new room
just four doors up the street
they lived in my mum and dad
for over thirty years
and a voice thrashing in the wilderness
an unstill enormous voice
is offering me this wisdom
*action's a solid bash*
*narrative a straight line*

*try writing to the moment*
*as it wimples like a burn*
*baby it's NOW!*

# Kinship Ties

He'd write *Neill*
airy flowing script
like an artist
– I especially liked the ∊
that was class

in our class
just now and then I'd have to write
my middle name
*Neilson*
– only one *l*
but it was like we were brothers
Neill and me
– in the Land of Ormeau
there was none closer

now that I've spelt out Neilson
like a guilty secret
no *ubi sumus*
let's leave it there

# The Rooks

*(Rimbaud)*

When the ground's as hard as rock
and the Angelus has gone dead
in each crushed village
Lord let the rooks
— those great clacky birds
sweep down from the clouds
onto fields and ridges

floppy crowd that bursts
into stony cries
the wind's bashing your nests!
— along yellow rivers roads
with their pitted Calvaries
over ditches and holes
you must scatter and rally!

turn in your thousands
over the fields of France
where the recent dead
lie maimed and broken
— in your clattery dance
our black funereal bird
remind us how they bled!

you sky saints in the treetops
draped on that dusky mast
above paradise lost
please let the May songbirds be
– for our sake who're trapped
beaten servile unfree
in the hawthorns' green dust

# Don't

*(after Heine)*

Don't mention it ever
– not when we're lying in bed
or eating dinner
– not when I'm making a meal
of your wet cunt
don't mention *Deutschland* to me

all that's been written and said
about homeland family slums
– I've gone right the way through it
so don't tell me I want to go back
– all the cards are there on the table
but the table's a long way away

we're just taking a holiday
for the rest of our natural lives
– like a tight big apple
we'll eat up ourselves and this city
so don't mention the skyblue Rhine
or that gospel tribe in the oakgrove

# Naïf

*Painting's the most primitive of all the arts*
was it Moore Kenny said that
or Davey Jameson?
I was anyway walking to work
either with Moore or with Davey
— Ealing Common 7 a.m.
our first time in London — kitchen porters
in a Lyons Cornerhouse
summer of miniskirts
summer of 66
— to think that remark
went unrecorded until now!
maybe I'm not grateful
that I had such friends

I'd write them and check it out
except we more than lost touch
— they both disappeared
they left Ulster for good
but in my heart of hearts I know
on the Cregagh Road and in Newtonbreda
those two are painting away
as an empty bus hammers on
past the Ormeau Park and the bakery
— *I thought I'd call by — just to say hello*

# Serial Lover in the Woodyard

It's pitchdark tonight
and the various pubs on the scars
have scraped their doors shut
so it's a very good time for him
— since they've no car
and must slope half a mile
back to her parents' house
— it's a good time to catch a hare
or a startled fieldmouse
now that his and her fingers
have become involved
and she fancies that this rather plain
practical man is her lover
— but if he likes to go
always from A to B why
this nighthunt this diversion?
does he want a grope and a kiss
or after all that beer
does he just need a piss?
— there the hare the hare not the mouse
goes jeuking and dodging
under the pooly arc lights
that make the watchman's hut
some dark Homeric shed
beside these huge pitchy piles
of raw bleak resinous timber
so bulky they look almost insane

– by night unstarred
and undissolved

of course like slashing the badger
this harehunt is a riddle
that's easy solved
before she can say *love stop it!*
or plead that he doesn't cadge
a vertical ride
just a couple of yards
from the main road's
odd dreary whang
– so it's cock into quim
a scrape on the fiddle
her hairy smile
as some rough magic
shakes and lurches her head
like a glove puppet

# Hegel and the War Criminals

The föhn was blowing
– a soft flimflam
as Hegel dug in the roots
of a liberty tree
– it was *populus alba*
the white or silver poplar
not the aspen
the trembling poplar
Hegel was nineteen
the Bastille had just been broken up
into doorstops paperweights and keyrings
and already Stalin's greatuncles
were busy digging pits

*

When Himmler visited Auschwitz
he noted that the crematorium
had been badly positioned
– foursquare and obvious
it needed concealing
so a screen of quickgrowing poplars
began to shoot up like rhubarb
– in summer sunlight the drizzly
almost tinselly light of the poplar leaves
flickered like chaff in a radar beam

During denazification
the Allies banned a cunning brownshirt
from giving classes and lectures
so Heidegger's fans
gathered in Freiburg
to hear a voice drone and spit
behind a net curtain
– half-pope half-fortuneteller
almost a popular figure
he rambled on about oaktrees
– you can still watch his acquittal
behind this text and that text

# A Poor Useless Creature

Jeremy Bentham
that sunny child
had a central heating system
installed in his London home
– the age of steam
was coming to a head
and Dr Bentham
held modern views
– they solved he said
the cold problem
– it was the task
of a longserving servant
to clear and stoke
the boiler at 5 a.m.
then he had to cook
a mutton or a bacon chop
to stoke the rational engine
that worked upstairs
– this solved the food problem
but one day sadly
when strapped for readies
he stole two silver spoons
from the dining – the feeding
room as it was termed
those two bald spoons
they solved his cash problem
but the hapless fellow

he didn't know
that he had fried
his final chop
– those spoons were numbered
tried and sentenced
– this solved the crime problem
he rode the cart
all the way to Tyburn
so he might give pleasure
even happiness of a sort
to a greedy crowd
that gathered with his master
to solve the pain problem
as they watched him drop

# Painting with Sawdust

This may sound insane
but if you take the way a saw
goes ripping and tearing
through a plank of pine or larch
– pine's a softwood while larch
is hard like bone
– if you listen to a saw giving out
those barking yelpy groans
those driven shouts and moans
that're wild as a drowning pup
or raw
like a wet shammy rubbing its knuckles
on a windowpane
– if you listen to the crazy chuckles
thrown out by a saw
in the heat of its only function in life
though to be strictly accurate that jagged blade
can't ever belong to what we call life
– if you reflect on the noises this knife
– this big thrawn toothy rather tinny knife
must make
then they might be a version those chuckles
of the way couples it's said
*are always going in and out*
*of intimacy*
which means that when the saw's
dogged panting

suddenly whoops screams and stops
– *chup!*
there's a change of tune
because now that its constant whuffing
has let up
one lover or the other must take a brush
not to paint a picture but lick up
what it seems such a pity not to leave behind
or leave new and untouched
– that tiny dune
of resiny sweet crumbs

# On the Windfarm

No thread to the wind
– no thread at all
it may weave clouds
may stretch their thunderheads
and their anvils
or bang like a hammer
– it can bang down really hard
like the *bora* in Trieste
that nearly broke Stendhal's arm
twice a week for a month

or it can soothe and sigh
for someone anyone
to smile and be happy
– *oh say you love her mr captain*
  *say you love mummy*
  *oh say it say it!*

but there's still no thread here
– contingent as speech
the wind's always guilty
of a total lack of backbone
and if you should seed
some prairie tornado
– drop dry ice from an airplane
that rational enterprise is doomed
the wind it veers off

to underline *storm damage*
in some other corner of the state
– as well ask that spinning demon
if he carries a condom

quite so humphs the windscholar
that wind it's history
history in the making of course
and solid as action
watch out or you'll reap –

don't give me that!
the windfarmer jumps in
pragmatic as the blades
on his aluminum mill
it's a willing worker the wind
why Benjamin Franklin
he was a windfarmer too
that kite and that key
they wouldn't never've
got off of the ground
if it hadn't been for the wind

no wind no sound
no life no culture
the grass would never grow
nor the clover neither
there would be no lithographs by Paul Klee
– no *Not durch Dürre*
no Paul Klee either

so the wind
it isn't so much everything
– rather spent phrase this
everything that is the case
as the rock on which
the true church of language
is forever building itself
then falling back down
the wind gives
the wind denies
the wind is a sermon
against itself
or the sound of Peter weeping

but it's still the wind's threadlessness
that gets on my nerves
the way it shifts and wavers
then blunders out into nowhere
– if the wind can be studied
is this feckless creature a subject?

no it isn't no
definitely not
there isn't a single form of knowledge
could ever net the wind
all we can do
is try to avoid
the heavy the hard
and the poisonous winds

those who try to confront them
are doomed to more than disappointment
– in Herodotus you find
that there used to be a small
a very small nation called the Psylli
who declared war
on one of the worst winds there is
the desert wind the simoom
it's a dirty heavy
a highly toxic wind
and the Psylli hated it badly
it dried away the water
in their stone tanks
it made their children ill

so the Psylli gathered spears bows and arrows
they stretched new ostrich skins on their shields
and practised slinging pebbles
– a prayer and a signal
they began their march
deep into the desert

the simoom duly came down
battle was engaged
a purple darkness hung
across the western corner
of the land called Psylli
– dark dark it was
on top of the noontide darkness
night inside night

come dawn
– a double dawn
come its fluttery suthery silence
no tracks in the sand
no Psylli
– all gone
gone every one of that tiny nation

had they only but spoken
to Franklin! cries the windfarmer
he'd have put on his mason's apron
he'd have beat that storm in the desert
he'd have beaten it hollow

## Palestinian Free State

One by one and two by two
they're blowing up the Arab houses
– houses? Arabs?
only shadows live here
and all that shadows need
in Eretz Israel
is one bright wall
to fall against

in the crystal dazzle
called Tel Aviv
there appears a city
of tight holiday homes
where all the settlers gather
in new store clothes
to praise the Leica's
optical hygiene
– what you see is what you see
soon that little puddle
of shadow history
will be a pocked dryness
and a wisp of steam
or a pocket state
where Michael Arafat
must whisper sadly
*is this the freedom
to win our freedom?*

# The Other England

Just as Charles Stuart
– that virus in the body politic
hid his rebel presence
in an oak tree
while troopers scoured the woods
after the battle of Worcester
so the evil essence
of all things royal
when it came to oust
the new republic
perched upon a tree
*the middle tree and highest*

now the shade of John Milton
asks how long will the loyal
citizens of Britain
go on bending the knee
to a scraggy vulture
that feasts on a spent tampon
and a dead dick?

# What's Natural

Taking a line out for a walk
ought to seem – well
second nature
like the way you laugh or talk
– though both speech and laughter
have to be learned
inside a culture
which means that when you take a pencil
and let the line go wandering
upon its lead
– or on its lead
there is
somewhere between a pun
and a tautology
this little yolky sun that wishes
it could just squeeze over the horizon
and chuck itself – splittery
splattery
all over the scrake
– the wheeze and piss
of dawn

# Priming the Pump

*Tin tack*
— lino floor
a flitch of bacon
hanging from a rafter
behind the counter

on a long saggy shelf
are several names
Powers Paddy Jameson and Bush
that sort of bond themselves
then selfreflect
— Cream of the Barley too
but that's nay good
maybe it's a stageset
out of Boucicault?
for it's earned something
— not that though

as for the pair of us
we're pitchpine cosy
Henry Snodden and myself
in this forgotten neuk
on the oh God
on the cloon of the stone circles
— praise be Henry nods
someone painted that buckin great portrait
of Rabbie Burns

all over the far wall
so a road – a famous road –
goes all the way
from Mossgiel to Melly's Bar
in Lettermacaward
– a dolphin road
  a mailroad
  a whaleway
  songs and spunkies say
  those things that are for real
  and that go somewhere

*

*Tick tack*
the chickering clock
more lino floor
more pitchpine
then there's the turfbox
where Madame Gonne
used plump herself
when she took tea
with the woman of the house
– Mrs Dorrian her name was
though above the door
it says   Ɗ.OƑAOLAƖƝ

the bar's between us
but her greatgrand-daughter hides
behind her fringe still
– *who else has hair*

*bayred as yours?*
your trinkling hair
*ack it's a pixture*

if I say about the weather
Concepta holds a mirror up
– I'm agreeing with you now
instead I say to her
this is a place of pure illusion
it's the phenomenal world we're in
– ack don't tell me we're in it
don't be saying *that* she answers
and goes out into the kitchen
I see the daylight yard beyond
a scruff of weed
she's out there feeding scraps to the dog
– by the cut of her shoulders she says
I'll not be staying in this clachan long
this yard that wall the bog the dunes
oh then the ocean
whatever it figures or could seem to mean
it's not my scene
me and my hair are leaving it

\*

*Nick nack*
a duff rhythm
just gristle and bone
or the fatty sweat of bone
a ball or a bald joint and socket

58

— the dog's chained to a drainpipe
it jerks and yaps and wuffs
as she scrapes out what's left
of Sunday's leg of lamb
— her da Henry says
her da's just had a bypass
— where? I ask him
— Letterkenny General
've you been there?
— I've been there OK
the day our Michael stuck his arm
right through a window
— the wee lad skinned it didn't he?
— *degloving* they call it
least that's the technical term
a barrister he —
— Stephen — ?
— aye Stephen Quinn it was
he told me doctors
doctors use it in the witness box
— that's money talking
— aye that's for definite

outside the dogchain
clicks and bips on the drainpipe
a beat but irregular
like a lanyard with a steel bit
flapping against a metal mast
or a flagpole
it's not OK it's not
it's an annoying

a listless sound
a sound without a pattern in it

*come on on in Concepta*
*come in and shut the dure*
*I can't stand the sound no more*
*of thon doggy's chain*

*oh don't you worry son*
*don't be getting anxious*
*something will come together*
*someone will play the taws*

*

*Dick dock*
than which
there can be nothing more basic
nothing lower or more blunt
than this particular verbal sandwich
– *dick dock*
  *than which*
warehouse sounds these
who'd ever want
to articulate them all together?
they belong
only in noteform
among shards and smashed pots

but because our house is full of dust
– chalky dust plaster dust old dust
a kind of dead but active *pousse*
expressed by filthy joists and floorboards
– because the whole place
is a grincing dusthole
I have to start somewhere

I've leant pictures against walls
rolled up the carpet like a standard
or the kind of rug you might spread
inside a tent
and I've taken down the curtains
so the room's become
brimful of new light
like a studio
a dustsheet's over the floor
as if for love or childbirth

– curtains carpets pictures
just get them out of here
the room must be as bare
as a carcase

now place the spirit level
on a flat surface
watch its little phallic bubble
shift and settle
this whole room's gotta be
under ma thumb!

but the dust hangs like a plague
like lice and flies
in the house of Pharaoh
and the iron lastcentury nails
are crude arrowheads
gnarled in some Black Country darg
for this is a pocket battlefield
a piece of the outside
inside four walls
where we cough dust
like the children of Israel
lost in the desert
we blunder about and see darkly
neither in the letter
nor the spirit either
I have to shove walls in
rip out the ceiling
and bash through the boast
the stud walls
these actions are solid
but Jesus
Jesus fuck
you could never put them in a sentence

in this shambles
— another packingcase republic
cables hang like entrails

chalk and string now
the ladder's triangle
a curved wooden mould

wet and ready
– in an oathless silence
the exercise of skill and reason
is more than both

and like chalk breaking on a blackboard
Jack Skryme overcomes
the scratchy curse of his name
to hurl slodgy dollops
of wet plaster at the wall
and we begin to see
– it's a boat docking
a shape
a graceful shape
faint and halfclassical
just beginning to stick

*

*Pick pack*
then the third and the fourth terms
*pock puck*
so *pick pack pock puck*
four sounds in their pecking order
waterdrops doing
what waterdrops do
– not a random haiku
nor a petty trouvaille
but their leisurely match
with leather on willow
or a finger plucking

this string and the next
while a kid listens
to the value
— *each tucked string tells*
of pure sound pure pattern
as they drop
in like Christ entering the temple

I am bespoken
oh ugly verb
I am bespoken
by these same sounds
— in Joyce's *Portrait*
how they break up
*the soft grey air*
and that equal fake
*slowly falling in the brimming bowl*
they smash them both
into conscience's
irreducible grit
— hardcore for a plinth
that becomes a temple
its classic flutes
and growth lines

so rip the ceiling
bash the walls
*things fail to spring*
*from nowt at call*
*and artbeginnings*
*least of all*

# Portnoo Pier

*Congested districts* you'd laugh
– crude grey utile
or as Locke says of the scriptures
a plain direct meaning
plonked next the rocks and the strand
and just as bald as Portnua

between this concrete quay
built about 1905 by yes
the Congested Districts Board
between this creature
and any idea of the beautiful
there's a very wide gap indeed

yet each time I walk down the hill
and notice how neatly
it echoes Noreen Cooper's
loyalist holiday blockhouse
this disappointed bridge
is home – home of a kind

for it whispers an ontic softness
to my namesake Tommy Pallin
in his slateroofed fisherman's cottage
– no electric no running water
just a Belfast sink and a pump
not a hint of any improvement

each morning in summer
he goes running along the concrete
then takes a header into the ocean
– a contented man Tommy
as he bashes the frameless mirror
*come on on in and join us!*

# American Light

We're right inside it here
way out on this saltwracked strand
at the mouth of the Gweebarra
an oysterfarm and seal primitives
on that sandbank's wet mirror
and though this light's moister softer
more jizz more quickchanging brightness in it
it is Cape Cod we're thinking of
– the wild China roses paths of clam shells
those little slights of fog
stuck in the firtrees

oh the daylight gods
– statues in some other capital
how we speed toward them
flaking down a bog road
in a hire car
each hump's like a ramp
like a sleeping policeman
– why not lean out and ask
if everywhere's stamped
with some civic emblem?
better make this a springboard
better we camped
round a turf fire
– see us drinking Jim Beam
and laughing our legs off

# Circumstantial

The hymen on the coffee jar
its gilt or silver foil
– likewise each shopping list's
an unfinished poem
that means *this young couple*
*have begun to live together*
though the twist is
if it isn't him it's her
keeps blocking the livingroom door

soon he can tell the foil she bursts
with her thumb
by the tatters round the rim
and if there's poetry in little things
– say bits of scrim
    that plosive lid
maybe also there's a small
phallic guilt
something niggly and annoying
that he'll never fathom?

# Going Back to the Sand Cabin

Like someone saying *I'll manage*
– which is what you've just said
you hear the phrase at a distance
sounding dull but cheerful
for you're the muggins
*qui doit quitter la plage*
to unpack the luggage
in the glazed the fixed the still
room you and one other
have rented
at the start of this long
displaced summer
– it's a framed piece of time
where already there's nothing
but a kind of dead
slackened feeling
like the floppy shine
on your baggage
for you would have to be
the balsa ever so cheery
one who takes on
this unspoken marriage
then stands looking
at two made beds
a hot planished sea
and the idea of doing damage

# A Taste of Blood

At long last he believes
that he's found a metaphor
to explain the way it always pans out
between the pair of them
– not the goose squeezing its golden egg
onto the livingroom carpet
not the poison tree
in the back garden
and not original either
it begins with the hinged shell
of an oyster
– if she's that flakewrinkled
that stone quim
its hackled undulant lip
and those barnacles and seaweed fronds
that must make it a version
of Botticelli's *Birth of Venus*
– if she's a clamped oyster
that may or may not have a liking for him
then he can only be a claspknife
that turns into Kinch
the fearful Calvinist
a hard penis
a hand writing
with someone else's pen
– no wonder then
that even in the act of love

the oyster won't open
and allow him to enter
all the deliciousness inside
– conned by his own boner
he feels like an arrowflake
crimped against the string
of Diana's tense bow
– that formal shape
will send him flying
for who would ever want
a spirit pranged like a knife
– a ghostblade
  a rustblade
  a jockteleg
to go charging
into the forests of her being?
but if he could only
dodge and shy between her lips
then he might melt into
her own quick melt

he lies on a lapsed futon
always losing and chasing answers
to his own question
there's a dirty spatter of rain
on the skylight window
its skittery sprinkle
falls on their amours
and she knows this morning there'll be blood
– blood and fuckyous
between them

# A Hard Sell

A honey infinite silk well
a sugarcane –
this is getting sensitive –
a sugarcane
or bamboo grove
a pair of shoes
splodging up a muddy slope
a piece of liver
on a bare fork
– I take the same seat in the train
an unchanging groove
and hope
at least I hope just now and then
to find out how
in the act of love
– a ramstam fuck
the split bamboo
has its own guilt
its own pleasure

## Sparrowgrass

Though it's different from goosegrass
to say it corrupts
from out *asparagus*
would be wrong
and though sparrows
don't like to be seen in long grass
*sparrowgrass* is its own concept
light and wavy like the smoky bush
that grows and grows
into a soft flumy
a feathery delicacy
when you let that strange
Greek or Roman head
drive its roots deeply
into a rich gritty bed

# The Bargain Bed

The one velvet headboard
– a double blank
has changed the shop window
into a public bedroom
where a no couple
sleep and make love
in the daytime

after dark the spotlights
warm for their non-entrance
this imaginary hotel room
with its furred headstone
its unstained mattress

## Loyal as Ever

About four every morning
I enter a short dream
about missing a boat or a train
a plane or a bus
– the message is obvious
*wake up! wake up! wake up!*
so here I am
with hours on my hands
and nothing to do or say or think
*what a waste!* says conscience
that stupid irascible unrelenting
dire tick in the brain
why won't it shut up?
can't I ever get rid
of this unstoppable thing?
just let me imagine
a small tin clock
with no hands
and no numerals either
– would you listen
to the blind scatter of its ticks
they're falling like seed
onto barren ground
where a long lost tribe
a tribe that mightn't exist

goes scouring the dust
for Onan's cock
and that annoying little clock

# A Last Gesture

In the case
of one particular painting
it's easy to guess
that a forest made me randy
– odd that
because power not desire
would seem more characteristic
of the Teutonic *Wald*
for isn't that Grimm fable
about the man whose nose grew and grew
a terrible warning
against unzipping your flies?

I recall the discomfort
of mud and cloth
the something annoying
about our makeshift bed
– my ass bare to the sky
my good coat on the grass
the sense – as she wiped her cunt
with a handkerchief –
of quitting a yolky bird's nest
while there filched into my head
the irrelevant question
why must Kandinsky always dress
like a concert pianist?
– though it was years

before he and I met
and became such friends

a day later I stretched a piece
of slightly scuffed airplane linen
on which I tried to enact
the desire of trees
their trunky leafbrush
their dance and sway

yes in war you improvise
there must be a chapter
in *Vom Kriege* about that
– coffee from acorns
gasoline from woodgas
rubber from whatever source

– so the artist Herr Clover
is like a nation at war?
then why on earth didn't you thrill
to our glorious dustups in the sky?
– inventing in a hurry
surviving barely
using whatever scraps came to hand
you still found the time
to sit back and jeer
at the Kaiser's sleek airplanes

eek! eek!
I don't want to listen
to such a plod plod person

I'm out on a drift
I'm losing the thread
— my examples were taken
from the second great war
o coffee gasoline and rubber
o acorns and woodgas
you're completely innocent as subjects
but is it such a pity
that I didn't know you ever?

my death was Swiss
— June 1940
so I missed
the Spitfires' high summer
— wave upon wave
doing their victory rolls
in a blue August sky
— each wingtip's honest curve
the oasis of each machine
how I could have painted them
on burlap or canvas!
but the disease I caught
it dried the fluids in my body
I had to quit smoking
and playing the violin
— *Hardship through Drought*
is my very last >—>o on the subject

# A Belfast *Bildungsroman*

*'And suddenly there came a sound from heaven as of a
rushing mighty wind and it filled all the house where they
were sitting.'*


As if I could write it out forever and ever
and me and the city be growing up always
pitching each fiction story or play
into that unscripted unwritten palm house
where the lord mayor ex-rigger plumber retired doffer
need never run out of gas or get stopped at a road block
for now the library shelves are chockablock with our
    consonants
and this great wee nest's packed with scaldies and egg sodas
we're being televised like wildlife *The Quaint the Cute and the
    Feral*
goes out on all channels 24 hours of the day
while up in the sky there's this huge transparent balloon
saying BELFAST DERRY it gets tighter and tighter
till it looks like bursting

                  who's stuffed on hot air?
who's been shooting their mouth off? can you tell us?
but the play is as innocent as seakale and needn't answer
for myself I want to lie on the ground like a humid pumpkin
– innocent postliterate no longer dirigible

my tiny cargo of civic angst floating down the lough
toward *that great and notable day* when the curtain goes up
on a stagestruck city soughing like a full house

# The Ivy Restaurant

*(for Matthew Evans)*

The wood panelling reminds me
of Ford Madox Ford's waistcoat
– that's nonsense though the common term
I suppose is *wainscot*
also *les Imagistes*
got drunk here once
for this is a literary lunch
(mustn't fall asleep)
where to make you squirm
I take up my knife and fork
to attack the deepfried brains
of a couple of dead sheep

# The Natural Order

The paddleshaped leaves on the banana palms
are shaped again in the stone temples
just as the pine forests deep inside Germany
have become gothic minsters
— *there's no escape* they say
*and there's no love*

we must bend the knee
in a stone forest or a stone grove
all that wood sap leaf
has crossed into our dreams like an army
everything we do
we do because it says so

the light of the desert though
is abstract and rational
— there's nothing natural
you'd need or want to imitate
so the mosque's this beautiful peaked
imaginary bulb

that's no bulb —
it stretches the sky
into itself the moon and stars
and might explain to me
why the writer
the precious secular

unconstrained deliberate writer
must suffer in a secret place
– alone he holds
his good right arm
and the state's liberties
unflinching in the flame

## Across the Howrah Bridge

On the banks of the Hooghly river
there's a huge banyan tree
the biggest in all Asia
– it's two hundred and twenty-five
or more years old
and ever since 1923
there's been a sort of hole
where the main trunk should be
– on our way north from Bhubaneswar
I found this sprawling woody creature
its branches propped by vertical
tubers – aerial roots painted white
and all supporting something with no centre
– a tree that isn't a tree quite
like the doubt in 'literature'

# Soldier and Packman

*(in memory Chanda Singh Khosa, 1908–93)*

The old havildar
makes angry in the courtyard
he takes an iron bar
to the water buffalo
then stops and lets out a roar
like a trapped bull
– not a week goes by but he casts out
his eldest son
and heaps curses on his daughters
– Gurbaksh Sarbjit
Manjit Srinderjit
them be no bloody good 'tall
Tarsem – Chin-DAY!
you'm get out!
now he calls for a chota peg
chota chota peg scherab!
but what he craves is a slug
from the litre bottle of Johnny Walker
that Swaran Kaur keeps by the rifle
in the padlocked press

we watch him lying
on a stringbed by the tubewell
every so often he sighs
– from Jullundur Canton
to Shipquay Street
from the railway sidings at Simla
to Small Heath or the Bogside
he's sent out naked again
– I'm a done man Tom
soon be dead – all finish!
him be your son Binday

dear father
old sinner
the risktaker the beloved
I watch your daughters cry their eyes out
then sift the ghat in prayer
for all that's left of our pitaji
what does it mean to forgive?
would you tell me?
– first ting you must be love
then maybe you'm die like me
shantih shantih

# The Sting

Anyone who has ever been hit
straight in the eye by a wasp
knows it's a bit like being poked
by the good Lord's little finger
– it resembles that moment
when the windshield binges
into quartzy toffee
the moment when it's only too clear
– too crystal clear –
that something has broken through
the riotshield that jigs
between self and reality
– it's simply a rehearsal
for the big finger
and it's what happened me
that summer afternoon
near Strabane
though as Tosser McCrossan would say
*if thon's all't hit you man*
*then you're lucky!*
or as you might add yourself
*I'm sure a wee sting*
*'ll leave your ego still intact*
but the fact is
this boy got stung
as we walked by the River Mourne
past Sion Mills

– I was staring at the yellow factory
dozens of windows and windowsills
all summery industry
when that stupid wasp
came zizzing across the river
and ruined my little ploy
for my heart it was set
on the tiny wee hasp
that showed through your cheesecloth blouse
– neither yoghurt nor cheese my love
but sugar brown sugar brown sugar
– but we couldn't dive down in the grass
for my sudden new patch of flesh
was hardly a turn-on that day
– just imagine
there'd have reared above you
the small bare ass
of that closed that stretched eyelid
blind and bald like a scaldy
or some indignant vulture
– *wouldn't you rather go back to the house?*
but as we continued our dander
you seemed relieved
and I felt – well – shrived
it was a pilgrimage of a kind
as we left that plonky
invented village behind
pushing through shives
of chippy sunlight
and the birds' *sip sip sip*
you with your brown lovely skin

me with my carrion eye
– then across the river
happened this curtainless manse
with a collapsed stone wall
and an orchard
all lichened and neglected
except that from out it the air
suthered a ripeness of plums
across the wimpling water
I closed my good eye
– what brushed my unkissed lips
like a prayer
was the blue grapes of Gilead

# Air Plane

Foursquare
a dead duck
– but a duck's not square
only if you say it is
say it and sigh

as for me I'd like to paint
or model a square duck
– *squak! squak!* it cries
its nest a bunker
its flightpath some buried cable
its eggs like building blocks
pure cubes of planed wood
or plastic bright blue plastic

why bother with such a creature?
I'll tell you why
– because so many poems
are like square ducks
that is they contrive
to be both tame and just

tucked out of harm's way
at the bottom of a column
these verbal machines
are definite
yes very definite
even when they're sad
they want us to love
their rigid waddle
their ticktock cries
the way they confront
our square earth
in its box of –
I should say *sky*
– in its box of air

# Cadmus and the Dragon

If Cadmus is the Age of Reason
                              – and he is
if Cadmus is the State
                              – and he is
if Cadmus is Descartes with a scalpel
                              – maybe so
then Cadmus must also
shadow Locke with his shovel
a shovel loaded with decaying sense
but always new and stainless
like the idea of rights
– rights not duties be it said
                              – yes brother


so Locke hires a surgeon barber
to make an incision
in the Earl of Shaftesbury's right side
for like a monstrous dragon
of superstition and formal piety
the suppurating cyst on the earl's liver
menaced English liberty
but the little silver tube
that Dr Locke inserted
gave one man life
and restored the nation's freedom

therefore Cadmus laid a conduit
in the body politic
which has to mean
that we're safe and secure
with Citizen Locke
– though they set spies on him
he worked
to bring ruin on the Stuarts
and plant an orange tree at the gates
of their state brothel

but if Cadmus is a subtle doctor
it also occurs to me
that Cadmus was present at a working lunch
in the Stormont Hotel
the winter of 90 or 91
– there was a civil servant on my right
and when I glanced at his left hand
a signet ring
cut with a tiny gold pentagram
was making its point quite silently
while beyond the picture window
the neoclassical gateway
the long straight drive
– it dips into the underworld
and that hollow muscly facade
were also making
much the same point
– so Cadmus is Sir Edward Carson
raising his bronze fist
against the twisty tail of Home Rule

– a theatrical gesture
he copied from James Larkin
who raised the dragon people
against their bosses

but let's say instead
that Cadmus is Willie Whitelaw
sitting at a bootshaped table
with the Spartoi
– they wear hoods
balaclava helmets
and dark glasses
– here Cyadmus
one of the hoods says
ye cannae sit in this coul chamber
wi a bare head
at a table that's shaped
like a Wellington boot
– put you a hood on
and we'll do business
for as Lévi-Strauss'd argue
*Cadmus is himself the dragon*
*and ancestor of the Spartoi*
or as it says in the Good Book
*as ye sow so shall ye reap*
so know ye this
Mr Kidglove Whitelaw
we're no Piltdown Planters
but the real autochthonous thing
– we're the Cruthin aye
a remnant of the ancient British people

who rose again in 98
in 1912 and . . .
ack I forget what date it was
but let Ballylumford
be our rath and fortress
we're not the 'RA
we're the 'DA
know what I mean like?
this is *Dadmus and the Cragon*
or *With the 'Da in Craigavon*

if this seems a shade slippy
what stays constant
is that our hero Cadmus
would appear to be masculine
he's all straight lines
he's rule and measure
a rigid prick
or as Carlos Williams notes
there are plenty men
*whose heads resemble*
*nothing so much as*
*the head of a dick*
which is how I came to see
John Cadmus III
sitting at the wheel
of his pickup truck
in a parking lot
outside a Safeway foodstore
in Tucumcari New Mexico
– he looked a tad

like Norman Schwarzkopf
the day he turned back
on the road to Baghdad

and though I spotted
– or say I spotted
his lookalike in Tucumcari
I should have changed the location
to Rockville
    Cementville
    Oilville
    Mechanicsville
for Cadmus is a grid person
who must imagine
not *amor loci*
not *dinnseanchas*
but the absolute antithesis of place
because he fears a parish dragon
some batlike mind
that's forever trying to snuff
a cosmopolitan enlightenment
– Locke's world of signs if you like

doing a steady 55
he admires all those high
blue boards along the freeway
how they say plainly
there is a rational liberty
that goes with cotton fields gumbo
and private property
this Cadmus

he'll have no truck
with the dragon of any particular place
he's dead frightened
of the monster that lives
in a cave overgrown
with branches and sally rods
— *a deep cave rich*
*in hot bubbling springs*
a funky cave
where the mud is edible
and tastes of tarragon

so it would seem that the monster
the Dragon Other
just has to be a fanny
— maybe *vagina dentata*
if that's your hairy fear
or the bottomless vagina
flying in the south wind
easy effortless as a windsock
infinite as language
or everything which is the case

so this monster's a giant fanny
o starry fig
o prickly
unpricked pear
o heavy moist musty warm wrinkledness
you belong in a gothic novel
— shave yourself and it's jacobin
scratchy as a cucumber leaf

else you're a barber's strop
a sea anemone
some tinker's budget
or a thatched bothie
– an extra skin so thin
it's no skin at all

watch Cadmus shiver
as he hears a voice crying
*you too will become a monster*
*you'll toss your bucket*
*into the bairns' well*
*and come back as fresh water*

now he imagines something
dry and itchy like a desert
warm and silky like the Nile
soft black sogflaky and
sweet as a pickled walnut
or brittle like a sea potato
furred on the tideline
yes this fleshy oxymoron
is an ocean
that's all ripples and taut muscles
it nips every cock in its pincers
and leaves behind
only a sagging fence hung with raindrops
piss sweat blood mucus
all the starchgreedy jism
they stream across
this prickly bed of tears

they enter this pouch
this tuppence hapenny
creased purse
— it's a quiver of desire
an oozy whooze
or a peppery paper wasps' nest

juiced and tightswelling
this blind cave
how it haunts the knight in armour
it'll smash every lance
that jigs into it
and mangle poor Boswell
who hides behind a rock
to try on a tricky condom
made out of a pig's intestine

or maybe this dragon
is a nation under arms
not a single hero with a name
it's the body earth
that turns out turds and babies
like loaves of bread
or it's the bloody earth
that rakes its own hills
*avec les crachats rouges de la mitraille*
and though its soldiers
spring fully armed
from out the grassy soil
only to hack each other
down to the last five

– the remnant
we console ourselves
that because Pallas
told them to observe a ceasefire
in order that Cadmus
might build Thebes
this has to mean
that we are all born of the spirit
and not the earth
though maybe the opposite
just happens to be the case?

# Basta

Would it – would it ever be
Year One again?
not that nondate no never
though in the end we agreed
to launch a reverse epic
in our chosen mode
– performance art
so *krangg! brumpfff! shlump!*
we took out the punishment block
the romper room
those wet black lanes
with sledges and crowbars
– it was a bop a real rave
as we chucked the grey
claggy remains
into a dozen skips
– our solid cheers as they swung
up onto truck after truck
our cheers rollicked the hillside
– *but is it credible*
*that by such thin threads*
*the great Leviathan was suspended*
*like the big weight to an eight day clock?*
– if you've seen armies hightailing it
out of dead land and desert
if you've heard a people hurrah
as the remnants hurtle

over a golden bridge
then you know the score
you see that the historians
can say no more
they can't ever believe
how below the dust and bits
— below the snapped electrodes
what we found was simply
a green field site
its grass almost liquid
like duckweed or cress
— so we waded right into
that watery plain
that blue blue ocean
and started diving and lepping
like true whales in clover

# That's It

Maybe because the light's so marine clear
in this new room
— this unexpected studio
maybe that's why the chest of drawers
placed in the dormer window
has to be stated like a proposition
so that its high bleached used pineyness
becomes a big bold drawing
that overpowers and oppresses
a man lying on a mattress
on an attic floor
— a man in the process of deciding
that he's begun to make old bones
and that because it's been dipped in an acid bath
the chest is neither one thing nor the other
for it belongs no more than he does
in this sky room above a city
— an old city that could be Florence but isn't

still suppose the mattress man thinks like this
— supposing I treat that chest as a novel
as a complete fiction?
then each drawer would be a chapter
which instead of socks or shirts
knitted jumpers or underpants
contained a sheaf of typed manuscript
— it'd be really neat that

for isn't the novel something which always fits
into its social space?
that functions in a room
is middleclass
and tries to make a bit of a splash?
and isn't prose a garment
a kind of social skin?
we wear it and it goes
— no we wear it and it stays
therefore prose is process
not a driftwood chest

all of which says only
that though I may be lying on a mattress
really I'm afloat
on a pool of light and illusion
yes light
and yes illusion